Work Sheets for Identifying and Closing Team-Gaps

RALPH H. KILMANN
AND ASSOCIATES

Distributed by
KILMANN DIAGNOSTICS
1 Suprema Drive
Newport Coast, CA 92657
www.kilmanndiagnostics.com
info@kilmanndiagnostics.com
949.497.8766

WORK SHEETS ON
IDENTIFYING TEAM-GAPS

Key Steps:
- Sensing Problems
- Defining Problems
- Deriving Solutions
- Implementing Solutions
- Evaluating Outcomes

**Plus the All-Purpose
Sanctioning System**

RALPH H. KILMANN

1. Sensing Problems

After every group member has completed and scored *Kilmanns Team-Gap Survey* (Newport Coast, CA: Kilmann Diagnostics, 2011), calculate the average team-gaps for each item on the survey:

Label & Code	Average Team-Gap	Label & Code	Average Team-Gap
Moving Forward	25/1 _____	Managing Differences	31/7 _____
Desired Norms	26/2 _____	Information & Boss	32/8 _____
Sanctioning System	27/3 _____	Respecting Egos	33/9 _____
Learning & Improving	28/4 _____	Being Valued	34/10 _____
Trusting Groups	29/5 _____	Sharing Ideas	35/11 _____
Trusting Managers	30/6 _____	Communicating	36/12 _____

Cultural Norms		**People Management**	

Label & Code	Average Team-Gap	Label & Code	Average Team-Gap
Understanding Goals	37/13 _____	Clarifying Priorities	43/19 _____
Involving Others	38/14 _____	Planning Work	44/20 _____
Defining Problems	39/15 _____	Managing Meetings	45/21 _____
Using Assumptions	40/16 _____	Time & Boss	46/22 _____
Problems & Boss	41/17 _____	Quieter Members	47/23 _____
Taking Responsibility	42/18 _____	Process Observer	48/24 _____

Problem Management		**Time Management**	

IDENTIFYING TEAM-GAPS

Once your group has calculated all of its 24 average team-gaps on the preceding page (item by item, rounded to the nearest tenth), sum the four columns for Cultural Norms, People Management, Problem Management, and Time Management. Then graph the four broad categories below, as you did for your scores on pages 30–31 in *Kilmanns Team-Gap Survey:*

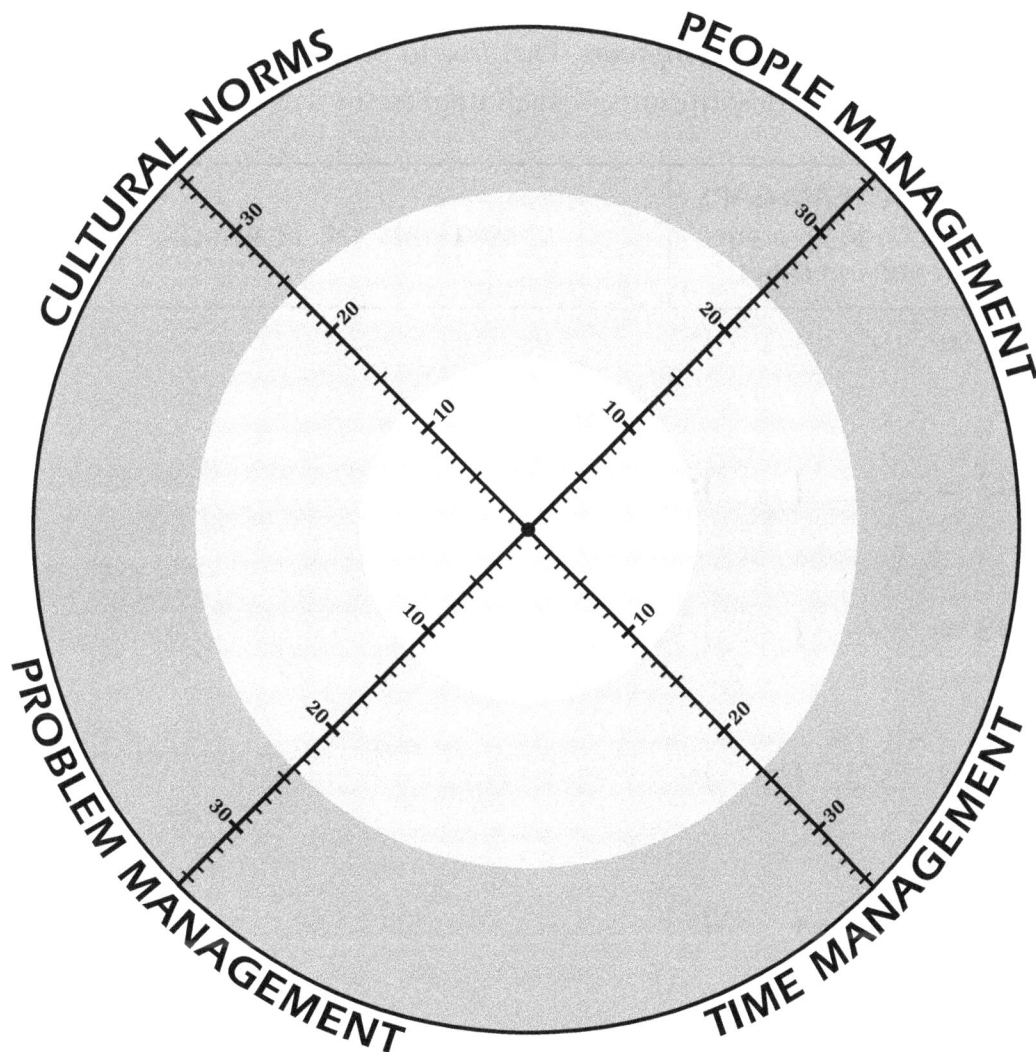

1. Sensing Problems (Continued)

Review all 24 average team-gaps. Rank-order five to ten of your largest team-gaps—depending on how many resulted in a group average of 2 or more. List the largest team-gap as #1, the next largest as #2, and so on—identifying each team-gap by its code number, group average, and item label (for example, #1 = 31/7 (4.1): Managing Differences; #2 = 44/20 (3.9): Planning Work). Then describe how each team-gap is *experienced* by group members: its **symptoms**. Feel free to provide more detail than is given by the brief descriptions of each item in the Team-Gap Survey.

LARGEST TEAM-GAPS Rank = Code (Average): Identifying Label	SYMPTOMS OF TEAM-GAPS
#1 = __/__ ( ):	
#2 = __/__ ( ):	
#3 = __/__ ( ):	
#4 = __/__ ( ):	
#5 = __/__ ( ):	

LARGEST TEAM-GAPS Rank = Code (Average): Identifying Label	SYMPTOMS OF TEAM-GAPS
#6 = __/__ ( ):	
#7 = __/__ ( ):	
#8 = __/__ ( ):	
#9 = __/__ ( ):	
#10 = __/__ ( ):	

2. Defining Problems

For each of your five to ten largest team-gaps, determine the *root causes* of the problem—using all the conceptual tools at your disposal (decision trees, assumptional analysis, dialectical thinking, and brainstorming). Try to pinpoint why and how each team-gap came into being and what keeps it alive. The better your group understands what is driving and sustaining each team-gap, the better your group will be able to derive and implement solutions that will close each team-gap.

LARGEST TEAM-GAPS Rank = Code (Average): Identifying Label	CAUSES OF TEAM-GAPS
#1 = __/__ ( ):	
#2 = __/__ ( ):	
#3 = __/__ ( ):	
#4 = __/__ ( ):	
#5 = __/__ ( ):	

LARGEST TEAM-GAPS Rank = Code (Average): Identifying Label	CAUSES OF TEAM-GAPS
#6 = __/__ ( ):	
#7 = __/__ ( ):	
#8 = __/__ ( ):	
#9 = __/__ ( ):	
#10 = __/__ ( ):	

3. Deriving Solutions

For each of your five to ten largest team-gaps, derive solutions that you believe will, if implemented properly, close the gap between actual and desired group functioning (or bring it within an acceptable range). Focus on those things (and people) that your group can control—either directly or indirectly. In this way, you will be able to implement your solutions in the next step of the process. Do not prescribe solutions for other groups and departments in your organization.

LARGEST TEAM-GAPS Rank = Code (Average): Identifying Label	SOLUTIONS FOR TEAM-GAPS
#1 = __/__ ( ):	
#2 = __/__ ( ):	
#3 = __/__ ( ):	
#4 = __/__ ( ):	
#5 = __/__ ( ):	

LARGEST TEAM-GAPS Rank = Code (Average): Identifying Label	SOLUTIONS FOR TEAM-GAPS
#6 = __/__ ( ):	
#7 = __/__ ( ):	
#8 = __/__ ( ):	
#9 = __/__ ( ):	
#10 = __/__ ( ):	

4. Implementing Solutions

For each of your five to ten largest team-gaps, develop an action plan (including tasks, people, and deadlines) for implementing the solutions that you derived in the previous step. Take into account everything you have learned about human nature and organizational culture. Test and revise your assumptions about what it takes to change and improve the functioning of individuals and groups in a complex organization. As a result, it is more likely that your solutions will realize their potential.

LARGEST TEAM-GAPS Rank = Code (Average): Identifying Label	ACTION PLANS FOR TEAM-GAPS
#1 = __/__ ( ):	
#2 = __/__ ( ):	
#3 = __/__ ( ):	
#4 = __/__ ( ):	
#5 = __/__ ( ):	

LARGEST TEAM-GAPS Rank = Code (Average): Identifying Label	ACTION PLANS FOR TEAM-GAPS
#6 = __/__ ( ):	
#7 = __/__ ( ):	
#8 = __/__ ( ):	
#9 = __/__ ( ):	
#10 = __/__ ( ):	

5. Evaluating Outcomes

For each of your five to ten largest team-gaps, how will you monitor the success of your solutions—both short term and long term? What results, signs, or symbols will convince you that each team-gap has been brought within an acceptable range? What will you do if you discover that your action plans have not, in fact, been implemented as intended? How will you adjust your plans to ensure that your team-gaps will close?

LARGEST TEAM-GAPS Rank = Code (Average): Identifying Label	RESULTS INDICATING SUCCESS
#1 = __/__ ( ):	
#2 = __/__ ( ):	
#3 = __/__ ( ):	
#4 = __/__ ( ):	
#5 = __/__ ( ):	

LARGEST TEAM-GAPS Rank = Code (Average): Identifying Label	RESULTS INDICATING SUCCESS
#6 = __/__ ( ):	
#7 = __/__ ( ):	
#8 = __/__ ( ):	
#9 = __/__ ( ):	
#10 = __/__ ( ):	

The All-Purpose Sanctioning System

What sanctioning system will your group use in order to close its team-gaps? What positive or negative sanctions will be provided when *victories* or *violations* occur? How will all group members break from the past and become organization-wide team players?

WORK SHEETS ON
CLOSING TEAM-GAPS

Key Steps:
- Sensing Problems
- Defining Problems
- Deriving Solutions
- Implementing Solutions
- Evaluating Outcomes

**Plus the All-Purpose
Sanctioning System**

RALPH H. KILMANN

1. Sensing Problems

After some time has passed, have each member take *Kilmanns Team-Gap Survey* a second time, so you can see what gaps have improved, stayed the same, or have become worse. As before, fill in the spaces below:

Item Label		FIRST TIME Average GAP		SECOND TIME Average GAP		Change (+ or –)
Moving Forward	25/1	_____	– _____		=	_____
Desired Norms	26/2	_____	– _____		=	_____
Sanctioning System	27/3	_____	– _____		=	_____
Learning & Improving	28/4	_____	– _____		=	_____
Trusting Groups	29/5	_____	– _____		=	_____
Trusting Managers	30/6	_____	– _____		=	_____

Cultural Norms		**–**		**=**	

Understanding Goals	37/13	_____	– _____		=	_____
Involving Others	38/14	_____	– _____		=	_____
Defining Problems	39/15	_____	– _____		=	_____
Using Assumptions	40/16	_____	– _____		=	_____
Problems & Boss	41/17	_____	– _____		=	_____
Taking Responsibility	42/18	_____	– _____		=	_____

Problem Management		**–**		**=**	

CLOSING TEAM-GAPS

Item Label		FIRST TIME Average GAP		SECOND TIME Average GAP		Change (+ or −)
Managing Differences	31/7	_____	− _____		=	_____
Information & Boss	32/8	_____	− _____		=	_____
Respecting Egos	33/9	_____	− _____		=	_____
Being Valued	34/10	_____	− _____		=	_____
Sharing Ideas	35/11	_____	− _____		=	_____
Communicating	36/12	_____	− _____		=	_____

People Management		−		=	

Clarifying Priorities	43/19	_____	− _____		=	_____
Planning Work	44/20	_____	− _____		=	_____
Managing Meetings	45/21	_____	− _____		=	_____
Time & Boss	46/22	_____	− _____		=	_____
Quieter Members	47/23	_____	− _____		=	_____
Process Observer	48/24	_____	− _____		=	_____

Time Management		−		=	

Team-Gap Comparisons

Examine the right-hand column on the preceding pages, labeled: **Change (+ or –).** Then, in the space below for each team-gap, summarize what has improved (+ change), stayed the same (zero change), or has become worse (– change) between the two times that your group completed the survey.

1. Cultural Norms

2. People Management

3. Problem Management

4. Time Management

1. Sensing Problems (Continued)

Examine the **second time** of the 24 average team-gaps. Then rank-order five to ten of your largest team-gaps: List the largest team-gap as #1, the next largest as #2, and so forth—identifying each team-gap by its code number, group average, and item label (for example, #1 = 31/7 (4.1): Managing Differences; #2 = 44/20 (3.9): Planning Work). Next, describe how each team-gap is *experienced* by the members of your group: its **symptoms.** Please feel free to provide more detail than is given by the brief descriptions of each item in *Kilmanns Team-Gap Survey.*

LARGEST TEAM-GAPS Rank = Code (Average): Identifying Label	SYMPTOMS OF TEAM-GAPS
#1 = __/__ ( ):	
#2 = __/__ ( ):	
#3 = __/__ ( ):	
#4 = __/__ ( ):	
#5 = __/__ ( ):	

LARGEST TEAM-GAPS Rank = Code (Average): Identifying Label	SYMPTOMS OF TEAM-GAPS
#6 = __/__ ( ):	
#7 = __/__ ( ):	
#8 = __/__ ( ):	
#9 = __/__ ( ):	
#10 = __/__ ( ):	

2. Defining Problems

For each of your five to ten largest team-gaps, determine the ***root causes*** of the problem—using all the conceptual tools at your disposal (decision trees, assumptional analysis, dialectical thinking, and brainstorming). Try to pinpoint why and how each team-gap came into being and what keeps it alive—especially for your most stubborn team-gaps. The better your group understands what is driving and sustaining each team-gap, the better your group will be able to close each team-gap.

LARGEST TEAM-GAPS Rank = Code (Average): Identifying Label	CAUSES OF TEAM-GAPS
#1 = __/__ ( ):	
#2 = __/__ ( ):	
#3 = __/__ ( ):	
#4 = __/__ ( ):	
#5 = __/__ ( ):	

LARGEST TEAM-GAPS Rank = Code (Average): Identifying Label	CAUSES OF TEAM-GAPS
#6 = __/__ ( ):	
#7 = __/__ ( ):	
#8 = __/__ ( ):	
#9 = __/__ ( ):	
#10 = __/__ ( ):	

3. Deriving Solutions

For each of your five to ten largest team-gaps, derive solutions that you believe will, if implemented properly, close the gap between actual and desired group functioning (or bring it within an acceptable range). Focus on those things (and people) that your group can control—either directly or indirectly. In this way, you will be able to implement your solutions in the next step of the process. *Be sure to reconsider any solutions that may not have been effective with your most stubborn team-gaps.*

LARGEST TEAM-GAPS Rank = Code (Average): Identifying Label	SOLUTIONS FOR TEAM-GAPS
#1 = __/__ ( ):	
#2 = __/__ ( ):	
#3 = __/__ ( ):	
#4 = __/__ ( ):	
#5 = __/__ ( ):	

LARGEST TEAM-GAPS Rank = Code (Average): Identifying Label	SOLUTIONS FOR TEAM-GAPS
#6 = __/__ ( ):	
#7 = __/__ ( ):	
#8 = __/__ ( ):	
#9 = __/__ ( ):	
#10 = __/__ ( ):	

4. Implementing Solutions

For each of your five to ten largest team-gaps, develop an action plan (including tasks, people, and deadlines) for implementing the solutions that you derived in the previous step. Take into account everything you have learned about human nature and organizational culture. Test and revise your assumptions about what it takes to change and improve the functioning of your work group—especially with respect to your most stubborn team-gaps.

LARGEST TEAM-GAPS Rank = Code (Average): Identifying Label	ACTION PLANS FOR TEAM-GAPS
#1 = __/__ ( ):	
#2 = __/__ ( ):	
#3 = __/__ ( ):	
#4 = __/__ ( ):	
#5 = __/__ ( ):	

LARGEST TEAM-GAPS Rank = Code (Average): Identifying Label	ACTION PLANS FOR TEAM-GAPS
#6 = __/__ ( ):	
#7 = __/__ ( ):	
#8 = __/__ ( ):	
#9 = __/__ ( ):	
#10 = __/__ ( ):	

5. Evaluating Outcomes

For each of your five to ten largest team-gaps, how will you monitor the success of your solutions—both short term and long term? What results, signs, or symbols will convince you that each team-gap has been brought within an acceptable range? What will you do if you discover that your action plans have not, in fact, been implemented as intended? How will you adjust your plans to close your most stubborn team-gaps?

LARGEST TEAM-GAPS Rank = Code (Average): Identifying Label	RESULTS INDICATING SUCCESS
#1 = __/__ ( ):	
#2 = __/__ ( ):	
#3 = __/__ ( ):	
#4 = __/__ ( ):	
#5 = __/__ ( ):	

LARGEST TEAM-GAPS Rank = Code (Average): Identifying Label	RESULTS INDICATING SUCCESS
#6 = __/__ ( ):	
#7 = __/__ ( ):	
#8 = __/__ ( ):	
#9 = __/__ ( ):	
#10 = __/__ ( ):	

The All-Purpose Sanctioning System

What sanctioning system will your group use to close its most stubborn team-gaps? What positive or negative sanctions will be provided when *victories* or *violations* occur? How will all members break from the past and become organization-wide team players?

Assessment Tools for the Eight Tracks Distributed by Kilmann Diagnostics

Kilmann-Saxton Culture-Gap® Survey

Kilmanns Organizational Belief Survey

Kilmanns Time-Gap Survey

Kilmanns Team-Gap Survey

Organizational Courage Assessment

Kilmann-Covin Organizational Influence Survey

Plus the Online Version of the

Thomas-Kilmann Conflict Mode Instrument

Plus These Training and Development Tools

Work Sheets for Identifying and Closing Culture-Gaps

Work Sheets for Identifying and Closing Team-Gaps

www.ingramcontent.com/pod-product-compliance
Lightning Source LLC
Chambersburg PA
CBHW081205270326
41930CB00014B/3307